QuoteOctopus.com

The best quotes

Publisher Contact

257 Swanston Street, Melbourne, VIC, AUSTRALIA

Email: hello@quoteoctopus.com

Social media: facebook.com/quoteoctopus

Acknowledgements

The team at Quote Octopus would like to thank our friends, family, suppliers and customers for making our vision of creating the highest-quality books a reality. Thanks for purchasing and enjoy the quotes!

This page is intentionally left blank

This page is intentionally left blank

A friend is one who has the same enemies as you have.

Abraham Lincoln

A house divided against itself cannot stand.

Abraham Lincoln

A woman is the only thing I am afraid of that I know will not hurt me.

Abraham Lincoln

All my life I have tried to pluck a thistle and plant a flower wherever the flower would grow in thought and mind.

Abraham Lincoln

All that I am, or hope to be, I owe to my angel mother.

Abraham Lincoln

All the armies of Europe, Asia and Africa combined, with all the treasure of the earth (our own excepted) in their military chest; with a Buonaparte for a commander, could not by force, take a drink from the Ohio, or make a track on the Blue Ridge, in a trial of a thousand years.

Abraham Lincoln

Allow the president to invade a neighboring nation, whenever he shall deem it necessary to repel an invasion, and you allow him to do so whenever he may choose to say he deems it necessary for such a purpose - and you allow him to make war at pleasure.

Abraham Lincoln

Always bear in mind that your own resolution to succeed is more important than any other.

Abraham Lincoln

Am I not destroying my enemies when I make friends of them?

Abraham Lincoln

America will never be destroyed from the outside. If we falter and lose our freedoms, it will be because we destroyed ourselves.

Abraham Lincoln

Any people anywhere, being inclined and having the power, have the right to rise up, and shake off the existing government, and form a new one that suits them better. This is a most valuable - a most sacred right - a right, which we hope and believe, is to liberate the world.

Abraham Lincoln

As I would not be a slave, so I would not be a master. This expresses my idea of democracy.

Abraham Lincoln

As our case is new, we must think and act anew.

Abraham Lincoln

At what point then is the approach of danger to be expected? I answer, if it ever reach us, it must spring up amongst us. It cannot come from abroad. If destruction be our lot, we must ourselves be its author and finisher. As a nation of freemen, we must live through all time, or die by suicide.

Abraham Lincoln

Avoid popularity if you would have peace.

Abraham Lincoln

Ballots are the rightful and peaceful successors to bullets.

Abraham Lincoln

Be sure you put your feet in the right place, then stand firm.

Abraham Lincoln

Better to remain silent and be thought a fool than to speak out and remove all doubt.

Abraham Lincoln

Books serve to show a man that those original thoughts of his aren't very new at all.

Abraham Lincoln

Character is like a tree and reputation like a shadow. The shadow is what we think of it; the tree is the real thing.

Abraham Lincoln

Common looking people are the best in the world: that is the reason the Lord makes so many of them.

Abraham Lincoln

Discourage litigation. Persuade your neighbors to compromise whenever you can. As a peacemaker the lawyer has superior opportunity of being a good man. There will still be business enough.

Abraham Lincoln

Don't interfere with anything in the Constitution. That must be maintained, for it is the only safeguard of our liberties.

Abraham Lincoln

Don't worry when you are not recognized, but strive to be worthy of recognition.

Abraham Lincoln

Every man is said to have his peculiar ambition. Whether it be true or not, I can say for one that I have no other so great as that of being truly esteemed of my fellow men, by rendering myself worthy of their esteem.

Abraham Lincoln

Every one desires to live long, but no one would be old.

Abraham Lincoln

Everybody likes a compliment.

Abraham Lincoln

Four score and seven years ago our fathers brought forth on this continent, a new nation, conceived in Liberty, and dedicated to the proposition that all men are created equal.

Abraham Lincoln

Give me six hours to chop down a tree and I will spend the first four sharpening the axe.

Abraham Lincoln

Government of the people, by the people, for the people, shall not perish from the Earth.

Abraham Lincoln

He has a right to criticize, who has a heart to help.

Abraham Lincoln

He who molds the public sentiment... makes statutes and decisions possible or impossible to make.

Abraham Lincoln

Hold on with a bulldog grip, and chew and choke as much as possible.

Abraham Lincoln

How many legs does a dog have if you call the tail a leg? Four. Calling a tail a leg doesn't make it a leg.

Abraham Lincoln

I am a firm believer in the people. If given the truth, they can be depended upon to meet any national crisis. The great point is to bring them the real facts.

Abraham Lincoln

I am not bound to win, but I am bound to be true. I am not bound to succeed, but I am bound to live by the light that I have. I must stand with anybody that stands right, and stand with him while he is right, and part with him when he goes wrong.

Abraham Lincoln

I can make more generals, but horses cost money.

Abraham Lincoln

I care not much for a man's religion whose dog and cat are not the better for it.

Abraham Lincoln

I desire so to conduct the affairs of this administration that if at the end... I have lost every other friend on earth, I shall at least have one friend left, and that friend shall be down inside of me.

Abraham Lincoln

I destroy my enemies when I make them my friends.

Abraham Lincoln

I do not think much of a man who is not wiser today than he was yesterday.

Abraham Lincoln

I do the very best I know how - the very best I can; and I mean to keep on doing so until the end.

Abraham Lincoln

I don't know who my grandfather was; I am much more concerned to know what his grandson will be.

Abraham Lincoln

I don't like that man. I must get to know him better.

Abraham Lincoln

I have always found that mercy bears richer fruits than strict justice.

Abraham Lincoln

I hope to stand firm enough to not go backward, and yet not go forward fast enough to wreck the country's cause.

Abraham Lincoln

I like to see a man proud of the place in which he lives. I like to see a man live so that his place will be proud of him.

Abraham Lincoln

I never had a policy; I have just tried to do my very best each and every day.

Abraham Lincoln

I remember my mother's prayers and they have always followed me. They have clung to me all my life.

Abraham Lincoln

I walk slowly, but I never walk backward.

Abraham Lincoln

I want it said of me by those who knew me best, that I always plucked a thistle and planted a flower where I thought a flower would grow.

Abraham Lincoln

I was losing interest in politics, when the repeal of the Missouri Compromise aroused me again. What I have done since then is pretty well known.

Abraham Lincoln

I will prepare and some day my chance will come.

Abraham Lincoln

I'm a slow walker, but I never walk back.

Abraham Lincoln

If I were to try to read, much less answer, all the attacks made on me, this shop might as well be closed for any other business.

Abraham Lincoln

If I were two-faced, would I be wearing this one?

Abraham Lincoln

If once you forfeit the confidence of your fellow-citizens, you can never regain their respect and esteem.

Abraham Lincoln

If there is anything that a man can do well, I say let him do it. Give him a chance.

Abraham Lincoln

If this is coffee, please bring me some tea; but if this is tea, please bring me some coffee.

Abraham Lincoln

If we could first know where we are, and whither we are tending, we could then better judge what to do, and how to do it.

Abraham Lincoln

If you call a tail a leg, how many legs has a dog? Five? No, calling a tail a leg don't make it a leg.

Abraham Lincoln

Important principles may, and must, be inflexible.

Abraham Lincoln

In giving freedom to the slave, we assure freedom to the free - honorable alike in what we give and what we preserve. We shall nobly save, or meanly lose, the last best hope of earth.

Abraham Lincoln

In great contests each party claims to act in accordance with the will of God. Both may be, and one must be wrong.

Abraham Lincoln

In the end, it's not the years in your life that count. It's the life in your years.

Abraham Lincoln

It has been my experience that folks who have no vices have very few virtues.

Abraham Lincoln

It is rather for us here dedicated to the great task remaining before us, that from these honored dead we take increased devotion to that cause for which they gave the last full measure of devotion.

Abraham Lincoln

Knavery and flattery are blood relations.

Abraham Lincoln

Labor is prior to, and independent of, capital. Capital is only the fruit of labor, and could never have existed if labor had not first existed. Labor is the superior of capital, and deserves much the higher consideration.

Abraham Lincoln

Let not him who is houseless pull down the house of another, but let him work diligently and build one for himself, thus by example assuring that his own shall be safe from violence when built.

Abraham Lincoln

Lets have faith that right makes might; and in that faith let us, to the end, dare to do our duty as we understand it.

Abraham Lincoln

Marriage is neither heaven nor hell, it is simply purgatory.

Abraham Lincoln

Most folks are as happy as they make up their minds to be.

Abraham Lincoln

My dream is of a place and a time where America will once again be seen as the last best hope of earth.

Abraham Lincoln

My great concern is not whether you have failed, but whether you are content with your failure.

Abraham Lincoln

Nearly all men can stand adversity, but if you want to test a man's character, give him power.

Abraham Lincoln

Never stir up litigation. A worse man can scarcely be found than one who does this.

Abraham Lincoln

No man has a good enough memory to be a successful liar.

Abraham Lincoln

No man is good enough to govern another man without the other's consent.

Abraham Lincoln

No matter how much cats fight, there always seem to be plenty of kittens.

Abraham Lincoln

Our defense is in the preservation of the spirit which prizes liberty as a heritage of all men, in all lands, everywhere. Destroy this spirit and you have planted the seeds of despotism around your own doors.

Abraham Lincoln

Public opinion in this country is everything.

Abraham Lincoln

Public sentiment is everything. With public sentiment, nothing can fail. Without it, nothing can succeed.

Abraham Lincoln

Republicans are for both the man and the dollar, but in case of conflict the man before the dollar.

Abraham Lincoln

Sir, my concern is not whether God is on our side; my greatest concern is to be on God's side, for God is always right.

Abraham Lincoln

Some day I shall be President.

Abraham Lincoln

Some single mind must be master, else there will be no agreement in anything.

Abraham Lincoln

Stand with anybody that stands right, stand with him while he is right and part with him when he goes wrong.

Abraham Lincoln

Surely God would not have created such a being as man, with an ability to grasp the infinite, to exist only for a day! No, no, man was made for immortality.

Abraham Lincoln

Tact is the ability to describe others as they see themselves.

Abraham Lincoln

That some achieve great success, is proof to all that others can achieve it as well.

Abraham Lincoln

That we we here highly resolve that these dead shall not have died in vain - that this nation, under God, shall have a new birth of freedom - and that government of the people, by the people, for the people, shall not perish from the earth.

Abraham Lincoln

The assertion that 'all men are created equal' was of no practical use in effecting our separation from Great Britain and it was placed in the Declaration not for that, but for future use.

Abraham Lincoln

The ballot is stronger than the bullet.

Abraham Lincoln

The best thing about the future is that it comes one day at a time.

Abraham Lincoln

The best way to destroy an enemy is to make him a friend.

Abraham Lincoln

The best way to get a bad law repealed is to enforce it strictly.

Abraham Lincoln

The dogmas of the quiet past are inadequate to the stormy present. The occasion is piled high with difficulty, and we must rise with the occasion. As our case is new, so we must think anew and act anew.

Abraham Lincoln

The highest art is always the most religious, and the greatest artist is always a devout person.

Abraham Lincoln

The people themselves, and not their servants, can safely reverse their own deliberate decisions.

Abraham Lincoln

The people will save their government, if the government itself will allow them.

Abraham Lincoln

The philosophy of the school room in one generation will be the philosophy of government in the next.

Abraham Lincoln

The probability that we may fail in the struggle ought not to deter us from the support of a cause we believe to be just.

Abraham Lincoln

The shepherd drives the wolf from the sheep's for which the sheep thanks the shepherd as his liberator, while the wolf denounces him for the same act as the destroyer of liberty. Plainly, the sheep and the wolf are not agreed upon a definition of liberty.

Abraham Lincoln

The things I want to know are in books; my best friend is the man who'll get me a book I ain't read.

Abraham Lincoln

The time comes upon every public man when it is best for him to keep his lips closed.

Abraham Lincoln

The way for a young man to rise is to improve himself in every way he can, never suspecting that anybody wishes to hinder him.

Abraham Lincoln

There is another old poet whose name I do not now remember who said, 'Truth is the daughter of Time.'

Abraham Lincoln

These capitalists generally act harmoniously and in concert, to fleece the people.

Abraham Lincoln

These men ask for just the same thing, fairness, and fairness only. This, so far as in my power, they, and all others, shall have.

Abraham Lincoln

Things may come to those who wait, but only the things left by those who hustle.

Abraham Lincoln

This country, with its institutions, belongs to the people who inhabit it. Whenever they shall grow weary of the existing government, they can exercise their constitutional right of amending it, or exercise their revolutionary right to overthrow it.

Abraham Lincoln

Those who deny freedom to others deserve it not for themselves.

Abraham Lincoln

To give victory to the right, not bloody bullets, but peaceful ballots only, are necessary.

Abraham Lincoln

Towering genius disdains a beaten path. It seeks regions hitherto unexplored.

Abraham Lincoln

We should be too big to take offense and too noble to give it.

Abraham Lincoln

We the people are the rightful masters of both Congress and the courts, not to overthrow the Constitution but to overthrow the men who pervert the Constitution.

Abraham Lincoln

What kills a skunk is the publicity it gives itself.

Abraham Lincoln

Whatever you are, be a good one.

Abraham Lincoln

When I am getting ready to reason with a man, I spend one-third of my time thinking about myself and what I am going to say and two-thirds about him and what he is going to say.

Abraham Lincoln

When I do good, I feel good. When I do bad, I feel bad. That's my religion.

Abraham Lincoln

When I hear a man preach, I like to see him act as if he were fighting bees.

Abraham Lincoln

When you have got an elephant by the hind legs and he is trying to run away, it's best to let him run.

Abraham Lincoln

Whenever I hear anyone arguing for slavery, I feel a strong impulse to see it tried on him personally.

Abraham Lincoln

With Malice toward none, with charity for all, with firmness in the right, as God gives us to see the right, let us strive on to finish the work we are in, to bind up the nation's wounds.

Abraham Lincoln

With public sentiment, nothing can fail. Without it, nothing can succeed.

Abraham Lincoln

With the fearful strain that is on me night and day, if I did not laugh I should die.

Abraham Lincoln

You can fool all the people some of the time, and some of the people all the time, but you cannot fool all the people all the time.

Abraham Lincoln

You cannot escape the responsibility of tomorrow by evading it today.

Abraham Lincoln

You have to do your own growing no matter how tall your grandfather was.

Abraham Lincoln

This page is intentionally left blank

This page is intentionally left blank

This page is intentionally left blank

This page is intentionally left blank

This page is intentionally left blank